D1495593

FLAVORS

To Hilton

with ink,

Mason Williams

MASON WILLIAMS

Doubleday & Company, Inc.
Garden City, New York

FOREWORD

If I had it to do over again,
I'd do it somewhere else.
How about your house?

CONTENTS

A variety of different flavors[1] that add up to one.

---

[1]The flavor of something is its taste, its atmosphere, its personality, its vibrations, what it feels like. We are evolving into new dimensions of language communication, a language made up of specific uses of the basic tools of word and image, a language of flavors. We now have whole stories that we use as single elements. In music, for example, one can compose with flavors as well as with notes. Bach, Villa-Lobos or the Beatles are specific and consistent flavors of notes and rhythms and therefore like single elements to create with.

A book is made up of words and becomes in essence a single word made up of many. We write with whole books as though they were single words. We write with flavors of words as words. Jesus Christ is more or less a single flavor, as is Hitler. All of W. C. Fields life and stuff add up to a flavor, and his flavor is part of the flavor of the twenties as is the twenties a part of the flavor of all America's history.

Love is a flavor, in fact, it's the overall flavor of time. God is a word for this flavor, which originally stood for the flavor of the weather of the Valley of the Nile as a word, and as an idea, the flavor that allows the most flavor possible of all the flavors possible. A pure almost flavorless flavor like water, one that is a basis for all flavors. We have kept the word, but we have lost the original experience, the original taste of God.

So, living here, In the Year of Our Word, 1970, I have a flavor that is made out of many flavors. This book will become a single ingredient in my eventual flavor as will my flavor, my whole life, become a single ingredient in the flavor of others. Hope you like it'ems.

MINCED MEDIA

DOGS

I think dogs are funny
barking
running
chasing
panting
wagging
that whole thing they've worked up is pretty funny
(Ever thought that dogs might be just dumb guys, that that's
the best they can do?)

STEWARDESSES

The mouths
Of Stewardesses
On Aeroplanes
Are the most standard
Mouths in the world
I stare agogged
At their springtime
Doublespearminted smiles
As they teach me all about
The oxygen m a s k

MY FIRST TRIP TO NEW YORK CITY

Today I arrived
In New York City
For the very first time
Age 29
6:45 theirs
3:45 mine

Rolling along
In the morning throng
Looking out the window
For the big skyline

I made a deal with myself a long time ago, I said
"I'm never going to go to New York City."
So I can say on my dying day
to the people around my bed
"There's one thing in my whole life I never did."
And then they can say
"What's that, kid?"
And then I can say
"I never did get to New York City."

So I blew the last thing
I ever wanted to say
By arriving today
In New York City

Monday, January 21st, 1968

CITY

City
Is when
A bunch of people
Get together
So they can start
Being shitty to one another
For being
Too close together

Then they want applause
For surviving the problem
Called city they've caused

Cities go
From one
To minus zero
They're put together well
Exactly wrong
Just like
Their throng

SONNET

In trying to compose a sonnet
As done by the finest of poets
I have to ponder upon it
Quite a bit even though it's
Simple to write one I've heard
Fourteen lines in all
The first line rhymes with the third
The second and fourth should fall
In rhyme in such a way
That a-b-a-b, etc.
So on and so forth say
Whatever the thought is to be
But it never turns out like I want it
Hey Nonny Nonny, Pissonnet

THEM SAND PICKERS

How about Them Sand Pickers,
Ain't they grand?
Sittin' on their haunches,
Pickin' in the sand.

Pickin' in the wet sand,
Pickin' in the dry,
Pickin' it fiercely,
Look at it fly!

Look at Them Sand Pickers,
Ain't they slick?
Some use their fingers,
Some use a stick.

Them seashore Sand Pickers,
Ain't they fine?
Sittin' in the sand,
Pickin' up time.

How to be a Sand Picker?
Don't need a ticket.
Find a bunch of sand,
Skootch down and pick it.

THEM STICKER GITTERS

How about Them Sticker Gitters,
Ain't they neat?
Gittin' them stickers
In they feet.

Gittin' them goatheads,
Gittin' them briars,
Pickin' them out with
Sticker Pickin' Pliers.

Look at Them Sticker Gitters,
Cain't they cuss?
Soons git a sticker,
Raise a mighty huge fuss.

Them tender-footed Sticker Gitters,
How they squeal,
Stickers in they toes,
Stickers in they heels.

How to be a Sticker Gitter?
Don't need a ticket.
Stick yer foot'n the weeds,
Let the stickers git it.

THEM BEAVER CLEAVERS

How about Them Beaver Cleavers,
Ain't they rank?
Cleavin' them beavers
Down on the bank.

Cleavin' they heads in,
Cleavin' they spine,
Clompin' them beavers,
Ever one they find.

Look at Them Beaver Cleavers,
Ain't they a shock?
Some use a ball-peen,
Some use a rock.

Them ever clever Beaver Cleavers,
Hidin' in the leaves.
Beaver comes by,
Gits a few cleaves.

How to be a Beaver Cleaver?
Ain't much to it.
Jist coldcock a beaver,
Reckon that'll do it.

I LOVE YOU AS THE CROW FLIES

I love you as the crow flies
Above everything else
Beyond the infinite
Dominions of distance
As far as away goes
I love you as the crow flies
Here

I love you as the crow flies
Straight into tomorrow
Beyond the timeless
Realms of past and future
As far as time goes
I love you as the crow flies
Now

I love you as the crow flies
Without caring why
Beyond the need
For rhymes and reasons
As far as why goes
I love you as the crow flies
Becaws

Stepping outside of her apartment
In the early morning stillness
I noticed how beautiful
The lines of a parking lot were

WHY THERE'S A WINDOW

Through the window
The wind bends
The green tassel tree
The gray bay waters lay
At the bottom of the day
The lumpy hump hill
Is very still
As not to dislodge
Its hodgepodge of lodgings
A double silver sky
Completes the why
There's a window

Over the red tiled spanish rooftop of the house across the street, a bright beachball shot high up in the air with no explanation. No shouts, no hands, no kids, no explanation at all; just part of a day in the life of a window.

KNIT PICKING

Bought eight pair of underwear today.
Why is a single piece of underwear called a pair?
Does that make a dirty pair of underwear also a dirty lie?
Come on, let's get this straight, O.K.?

James Brockman
SANTA MONICA, Calif., May 31 (AP).—James Brockman, 80, songwriter whose "I'm Forever Blowing Bubbles" was a hit, died May 22, it was disclosed yesterday.

FRANK, THE ———— BANDIT
(Fill in the ————s with ————.)

Frank's mind was ———— as he entered The First National ————, except for the fact that he knew he was going to rob it. (The ———— that is.) He filled out a ———— deposit ———— with the words "KEEP YOUR ————ING MOUTH SHUT. THIS IS A ———— ROBBERY. PUT ALL THE ———— NOTES YOU'VE GOT INTO THIS SACK. THESE AIN'T ————S IN THIS PISTOL." (But they were.)

The stunned ———— teller just stood there with a ———— look on her face. Frank fired a ———— to make her hurry up, but she ————ed out. The other ————ers went crazy and started screaming and yelling, so Frank got his ———— out of there, leaving the loot behind. Frank, The ———— Bandit had ————ed up again, drawing a complete ————.

The shortest distance between two points is: ⟵

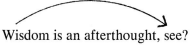

Wisdom is an afterthought, see?

Admit your weaknesses
And be therefore
Stronger

WeAK

THE
DA-DA
TRILOGY

I
THE PRINCE'S PANTIES

II
THE EXCITING ACCIDENT

III
THE LAST GREAT WALTZ

IV
THE TOMATO VENDETTA

V
(WHISTLE) HEAR!

THE PRINCE'S PANTIES

There was once a prince who
Acted strangely in that
He thought life was stupid
And it was for him, so
He made up a world in
Which he liked the things we
Like, but he had different
Reasons why he liked them
He liked butter for its color
He would order toast and color
Waitresses confused would utter
"Sir, I've never heard
Of toast and color."
He'd get angry and
Begin to choke them
The law would come and
They'd arrest and book him
So his life was
A mess of trouble
Still he kept it up

He had dogs, a hundred
Cocker spaniels and he
Called them panties 'cause they
Did that mostly and he
Did not care at all if
They would bark and fetch sticks
Run and jump, roll over
And play dead tricks, no he
Liked them only for their
Panting, so he would
Run them ragged, but one day
They got fed up and
Chased the prince right up
Against a fence and the
Prince was eaten by his panties

THE EXCITING ACCIDENT

Late one night a bunch of us
Were hungry for a snack.
We stopped at a nightery
And sat way in the back.
We all ordered stuff to drink,
Some coffee, milk and cokes,
And conversed on worldly things
And told some dirty jokes.
We weren't causing trouble
But then suddenly a man
Jumped up from his counter seat
And, pointing with his hand,
Said to us with narrow eyes,
His voice was like a hiss:
"Sadness," he said, "is the mortar
Between our happiness!"
Then he turned and ran
But accidentally careened,
And knocked over with a crash
A gum ball machine.

Gum balls spilled all over the sidewalk.
Some rolled off the curb,
No one seemed to care about that,
No, no one said a word.
"What the heck was eating him?"
We wondered in the lull.
This is not a true tale, but
Who needs truth if it's dull?

THE LAST GREAT WALTZ

$\frac{4}{4}$ Johnathan Double U Astor
Was a master dancing man.
He danced the day that he was born,
His parents thought him grand.
The tango and the samba
He did with great elán,
But most he liked to dance the waltz
Until the break of dawn.

$\frac{3}{4}$ "I like the waltz,
It has its faultz,
For there are some dances more fancy.
I like the waltz
Simply becaultz
It makes me feel so dancy."

$\frac{4}{4}$ One day he got an invitation
To a ballroom dance,
And he decided to accept
For he might get a chance
To dance with lovely ladies
With perfume in their hair,
Or even fat and ugly ones,
He really didn't care.

$\frac{4}{4}$ But at the ball the same old story
Made his evening grim.
He was a perfectionist
And none would dance with him.
So he thought he'd just go home
And write an anguished poem
But on his way out he saw a girl
Dancing all alone.

$\frac{3}{4}$ "I like the waltz,
It has its faultz,
It's not much fun unless danced by two.
I wish I knew
Somebody who
Would waltz with me . . . I'm so Blue Danube."

$\frac{4}{4}$ She was waltzing by herself
There in a little nook.
He quietly walked to where she was
To get a better look.
She was a little different
From either you or me,
For she did not have two good legs,
She had one, two, three!

$\dfrac{3}{4}$ "I like the waltz,
I have my faultz,
I have three legs, but I'm in good health.
I like the waltz
Mostly becaultz
I have to dance all by myself."

$\dfrac{3}{4}$ "First the right foot,
Then the middle foot,
Then the left foot, then I repeat.
I make no mistakes,
I've got what it takes,
One, two, three feet for waltzing is neat!"

$\dfrac{4}{4}$ Johnathan Double U Astor
Asked her, "Would you like to dance?"
To which she answered,
"Yes."
So they began to waltz
In a most peculiar way.
She had three legs, he had two,
And they were heard to say:

$\dfrac{5}{4}$ "We like the waltz,
We have our faultz,
But we are happy for the first time.
Though we are different,
We took a chance,
And found true love in an off-beat romance."

THE TOMATO VENDETTA

This song's about the Tomato Vendetta
And the tale of a man who let a
Hate for tomatos cause him strife
He lost his job, wife, home, car, kids and life

He'd go downtown to buy some groceries
He went because his family was hungry
He always bought bread, meat and potatos
But he wouldn't touch those ugly tomatos

He didn't know why he hated tomatos
They just were as ugly as far as ugly goes
There in the store, when no one was watching
He'd set melons on them and laugh at their squashing

One night after shopping and on his way home
His loathing for tomatos cut to the bone
He just couldn't stand the strain anymore
He vowed to destroy the tomato horde

He turned around and viciously hopin'
The grocery stores would still be open
His eyes grew cold, for he was a man
Whose moment of truth was close at hand

All over town in every store
Tomatos were hurt and spilled on the floor
Big melons and turkeys and large sacks of grits
Were dumped on their sections to mash them to bits

At the last store he finished his plan
But on his way out a delivery van
Full of big ripe tomatos drove in and hit him
Tomato Vendetta had claimed its victim

The incident of the **Tomato Vendetta**
Caused a sensation, it was something that the
Public could relish and readily snatch up
Popularly known as the tomato catch up

(WHISTLE) HEAR!

There was once a man who couldn't do much
Everytime he reached, he couldn't touch
Everything he said was so much wind
So he'd just stand around and listen in

He heard
Song talking people
People talking songs
Singing people talk
Talking people sing
All those people
Talking and singing
About all those things

He heard everything that people had done
But when you've heard them all, you've just heard one
So he began to listen all around
To a wider spectrum of sound

He heard
Thud, bang, a-beep-beep, click
Boom, chuk-a-yuk-yuk
Whirrrr, tick-tick
Boing, buzz, honk-a-ding-ding
Rumble-bump-a-bip, crack
Ring-a-ling-a-ling

When he'd done heard all there was to do hear
He began to search for something new here
There's more silent things than that sound something
So he listened to the shades of nothing

He heard
Rocks, sky
Sun, eyes
Wood, water, earth
Time flying by
Skin, grass
But none surpassed
The sweet sound of love

But things began to get a little bit weird
What he heard no one had ever adheared
Since silence sounds more or less the same
His mind played a silent little game

He heard
Rocks in the sky
The sun in his eyes
Wood, water, earth
In the time flying by
The skin of the grass
And when he heard love
Honey ran out of his ear

(Whistle) Hear!

AUTOBIOGRAPHY

The first car I ever drove by myself was a 1936 Chevrolet 4-door sedan. I was 14 years old. It was one of my stepfather's cars. He was a truck driver, so we always had at least three or four cars that he tinkered with sitting in the yard. He swapped and traded them all the time. They sort of came and went like stray dogs.

I had started watching people drive to learn how myself, and one day while everybody was gone, I thought I'd sneak a try. I got in the car and started it up. The engine seemed to be running fast, but I thought it would probably slow down after I put it in gear. I pushed in the clutch, put it in reverse and let the clutch out. The gear grabbed and the car took off backwards all the way across the yard and crashed into a tree. It knocked off the trunk lid, broke the back window and bent up a bunch of other stuff underneath. I found out later that my stepfather had been working on it and had left the dashboard throttle out all the way. I spent the afternoon staring at what I'd done, walking off and coming back. I must have looked at it 40 times from 40 different angles, trying to see it so it didn't look so bad. There was just no way to glue it back and hide it.

I had to let enough time go by before I brought up learning to drive again, but I finally eased back into it, and my mother started letting me drive on deserted logging roads until I learned how. We had a 1942 Plymouth that I used mostly, I wasn't allowed to drive the good car, the '49 Oldsmobile. I became little Mr. Goody-Goody around the house, I was suddenly trustworthy, obedient and reliable, especially when it came time to go to the store or run an errand.

The Plymouth more or less became mine virtually by its possession of me. I took care of it all the time. I guess it was to me like my mother's flowers were to her. It was the first thing I checked on every morning.

I did a lot of firsts in that car, my first feel of big-time real-life independence, (I would grin out loud and look at old hot stuff me in the rear view mirror), my first sallies into neighboring towns, my first Sally in a back seat, and my first drunk. (A friend drove me home in it, and I got sick and threw up all over the door. It messed up the paint job. I was so hung over the next day, I didn't bother to wash it off and the sun baked the streaks into the paint.)

It was also my first adult artistic statement. I bought everything I could afford from the Sears' Catalogue Auto Accessories Section and put it on the car — reflectors, mud flaps, a steering wheel knob, a dashboard compass, chrome smitties, half moons, spinners, fender skirts, silver stars and decals. It was a jukebox on wheels.

I also had my first accident in it. Me and three friends ran out of gas one night on the highway that runs through the middle of town, and we were trying to coast down a hill to a gas station. Suddenly a car came up over the hill behind us. He must have been coming about 70. My friends saw it out the back window. They all whooped and ditched in three different directions, but I stayed with it. I braced myself and watched the lights get bigger in the rear view mirror. When it hit me, the front end lifted up into the sky and I remember noticing how clear the stars were through the windshield. I didn't get hurt, but the guy behind me did a little bit. He hit his head on the windshield, but he was drunk, so I guess that's what saved him.

The '42 was totaled. The frame was bent, they said, and couldn't be fixed. I didn't see why. It seemed like a waste of a good car to me. I didn't like the way people talked about it — it was like a horse with a broken leg they wanted to shoot.

I bought my first car when I was sixteen. I had had a paper route in Oklahoma City in the 9th grade and had saved up two hundred dollars to buy a car with when I got old enough. Oklahoma was still a dry state then, and an uncle of mine had a big garage building that he stored cars in that had been confiscated from bootleggers by the state troopers. Every now and then they would auction off the cars to the general public or to used car dealers. I asked my uncle which ones he thought might go for around two hundred dollars. He pointed out the ones he thought might sell in my range. They all looked like ordinary cars on the outside, but most of them had been souped up or altered in some way for booze hauling. Of all of them, the only one I could see owning was a black '48 Ford. My uncle told me that the auction would probably take place while I was in school, so I gave him the money to bid on it for me.

The day of the auction was a drag in school, I just knew some loaded used car lotter was going to steal my car — two hundred dollars was my limit. After school I ran over to my uncle's garage and there she was. The bidding had gone all the way up to $216, but he had gone ahead and got it anyway.

The car was great. It had a full race 59-AB Block Mercury engine, which I mentioned to everybody — even girls. I didn't know why that was good to mention, but hot rodders always whistled when I told them about it, so I just told everybody. It was really fast. Sometimes I'd drag somebody for a couple of blocks, but mostly I used it just to roar around town, and school parking lots or burn rubber in front of girls.

It had truck springs in the rear end. They had been put in by the bootlegger to raise up the back so that when it was hauling a load of whiskey it didn't look weighted down. The only drawback to this was that without a load, the rear end stuck way up in the air. I left it this way for a while, because everybody used to say how dumb it looked, and then I'd hit 'em with the big story about how it used to be an outlaw's machine. But later on, I got to where I disliked the looks of it myself. You could see everything underneath. It felt like everybody was looking up my car's dress, so I stacked about four hundred pounds of concrete block in the trunk to level it off.

I really worked on keeping my car sharp looking during my junior year in high school, but when I got to be a senior, I started tearing around, doing all that senior stuff, and the car began to wear out. As it did, so did my feeling for it. I guess I was developing the attitude toward it that I've seen a lot of guys have toward their things, especially their wives. When they start to fall apart and get ugly, you kick it around a little bit to hurry up and finish it off. I didn't like it when it began to show me up as not having what it takes to take care of it. It got to the point where I'd drag anybody or give any girl a ride, and when it wouldn't work good I'd bang it around.

I finally finished it off one Saturday morning. A girlfriend and I had decided to drive to Dallas just to see if we could make it there and back. We were driving down a four lane doing a little light courting. I had the hand throttle out and my feet upon the dashboard, steering with my elbow. The car was rolling along on it's own at about 50. There wasn't anything but a cattle truck way up the road and it seemed a long way off. I leaned over and kissed her a long one. When I finally looked up, we were right on top of the truck. I straightened up, but missed the brake and hit the clutch. The car just sort of sailed into the rear end of the truck. It wasn't a hard hit, but the cows in the truck went crazy, mooing and banging the side boards. They were probably stampeding, but you know, how far can you go in a cattle truck?

I pulled over and stopped the car and the truck pulled off the road up ahead. The driver jumped down out of the cab, came running back and asked if anybody was hurt. I said no and started lying about how a loose piece of floorboard had made the gas pedal stick. He listened to all of it with one ear while looking things over. His truck seemed to be O.K. He quieted the cattle down a little bit, then came over, grinned and said, "Well, what do you want to do?" I said, "Well, I'd just soon skip it if you would." He said, "O.K. by me," grinned again, said goodbye and that was it. He fired up the truck, waved out the window and pulled away.

We watched him drive off, then I took a close look at my car. It wasn't hurt too bad, actually, one of the fan blades had broken off and gone through the hood like a piece of shrapnel, and the grill had been pushed in just enough to give it a dumb "duh" smile, but it would still motate. However, there was a lot of fresh green cow shit splattered all over the hood and windshield. I walked over to the side of the road, picked up a stick and scraped off the windshield enough to see out of. We had to drive back to the city pretty slow, the odor overtook us if we got going too fast.

I was in a total teenage pout. It was more than I could take. The car was just not good enough for me anymore. It was divorce. I put an ad in the paper and sold it to some guy with red hair for fifty bucks.

I didn't have a car for about three years after that. I went out to L.A. with Ed Ruscha to go to school or whatever, and we drove it in Ed's car, a 1950 Ford 4-door Custom sedan. I remember it had a fancy white steering wheel, used a lot of oil, and had the ride of a big soft bed. But it was Ed's car, so I won't go into it.

I only lived in L.A. for eight months, I didn't like it very much. Not having a car was probably the big reason, you're really stuck without a car in L.A. I went back to Oklahoma City to go to Oklahoma City University, and I didn't have a car there either, but it didn't matter. Oklahoma City was a little more of a walking town than L.A. Besides, you don't really need a car in college; somebody always has one and if they don't, you just hitch-hike or skip it.

The next car I got was one I got when I got married. I had dropped out of college because of money and folksinging, I had taken all the good stuff anyway, and was living in Tulsa, Oklahoma singing at a coffee house/art gallery type place — just coasting. I asked a girl I had met at North Texas State up for a visit one weekend and the way things turned out, we decided we had to get married.

I bought the whole shebang, the ring, the suit, the church wedding and the honeymoon car. It was a 1951 2-door, 2-tone light green and grey Chevrolet. It was clean and ran good, which is all you need for a honeymoon.

During the time I was married, I was serious about my car. It was my family badge. I kept it clean, washed and waxed and in good running condition. I wasn't a kid anymore, so I adopted my father's attitude toward his car. It was a married man's work car, so watch out.

The baby came while I was in the Navy. As soon as I could, I went back to Oklahoma City to bring the family out to California where I was stationed. We drove the '51 Chevy with the back seat and trunk full of everything we had. We lived on Coronado Island. Every work day, I joined the daily squared-away parade to the base.

There were no romantic illusions connected with this car. The baby seat probably did more to keep it real than anything else. My attitude was, "Who cares as long as it gets you where you're going." I even said it.

It was a good little car though, it went to work, to the store, to the doctor and all those thousand places and finally to my wife. We didn't split up mad or anything. She wanted to go back to college and become a teacher, so I gave it to her and she used it for a couple of more years.

After serving my time in the military and trying to be married at the same time, I decided it was high time I went back to Oklahoma City to finish college. I had been a folksinger after working hours in the Navy. I played for coffee houses, bars, PTA meetings, you name it, to make a little extra money. So to pay for school and stuff and to help my ex-wife out a little bit, I did the same thing in Oklahoma City — selling music by the pound. I worked as much and as late as I and school could take, and finally got enough together to make a down payment on another car. I bought a fine looking '56 green and white Ford *Dreamliner*. It was seven years old, but still pretty far uptown for me. I was itchy to get living after the service, so we took off. I began driving anywhere for any reason — all of which were girls. I had such a good time having such a good time that I ran out of money and had to take a folksinging job for a full week in Denver at a club called The Exodus. I was only going to take 10 days off altogether because of school, but I did, however, decide to go by and see a girl I knew in Iowa City on the way, which is only about 1400 miles out of the.

I always drove straight through to wherever I was going, so I went from Oklahoma City to Iowa City without stopping. I remember being about to bust from grinning, the road felt so good after having been tied up and down for so long. I zoomed and sang all the way, yelling songs out the window.

I got to Iowa City, but had an argument with the girl — I surprised her she said. I slept on the floor for a couple of hours, then got up and drove on to Denver.

The car was a new, old time religion, a revival of freedom. I was ready to go anywhere, anytime, anyhow, so I did. After the job, I went up to Aspen with a bunch of people I'd met at the club and ended up spending all the money I'd made for school. I had to go back through Denver to borrow enough to get home on. I decided to go back by Iowa City and surprise that girl I knew there once more. She couldn't believe it was me again, so I stayed around a couple of days to show her, but after awhile I got tired of her sticking her independence in my face instead of what I wanted, so I went on home.

On the way, the car started falling apart; it leaked oil, whined and ground finally to a halt when the generator went out in Kansas City. It was late at night and I had a hard time finding a place open to fix it. I finally found an all night filling station that did emergency repairs. The guy put it up on the grease rack and started working on it. He had to wait on his gas customers and work on my car inbetween. I hated that little drive-over hose bell.

I got tired of shuffling around the station and looking over the fan belt assortment for the hundredth time, so I climbed up on a work bench, opened the door and took down my guitar to pass a little time with. I left the door open.

I got absorbed in playing and talking to the mechanic and when he got finished and started to lower the car, he didn't realize and I forgot to tell him that the door was open. It caught on a work bench, broke the bench and almost tore the door off, it had a big V-shaped dent in the bottom of it and it was sprung and wouldn't close good either. Neither one of us knew whose fault it was, or who was hurt the most, so I just looked up in the sky a little bit, then paid him for the work and drove off.

By the time I got back to Oklahoma City, the car was a mess. I was pure-dee pissed off. I went back to the Ford dealer who had sold it to me and exploded all over him for selling me a car without telling me the truth about what shape it was in. He didn't really give a shit and like most Ford dealers, had the art of kissing you off down pat. I thought about blowing up his lot, like everybody else probably does, but like everybody else I didn't, because I couldn't figure out a way to get away with it. (I sincerely believe that used car dealers, and Ford dealers especially, are the re-incarnated small time saloon owners of the old West.)

There was no way I could catch up on my school work. I'd been gone 20 days from school instead of 10, so I decided to pull up and put it together some other way somewhere else. A music publisher in L.A. had just offered me $200 a month to come out and write songs, so I got an advance from him to get the car fixed, dropped out of school officially, loaded up my junk and took off for California. I got there on the 8th of January, 1964.

For the next year and a half, I was a folksinger operating out of my car, the door of which I never did fix. I lived at a place in L.A. with Ed Ruscha and his brother, Paul. But mostly I was on the road, working the folk club circuit and a chain of Holiday Inn's in the southwest as far down as Laredo, Texas and as far out as Huntsville, Alabama. I treated my car like it was a P-51 Flying Tiger flying missions over China. Everywhere I went was a raid of some kind. It was me and this car against the odds. I put about 100,000 miles on it in that year and a half. I took good care of the motor and the mechanical stuff, but I didn't waste too much energy on the looks. There were always beer cans and pop bottles rolling around in the floorboards among the chewing gum and candy bar wrappers, and it usually had a pretty good coat of red road mud caked on the ouside.

About ½ way through 1965, I started to find enough work around L.A. and Hollywood, so I quit going on the long road trips. Being around Hollywood began to rub off on me. I started getting a case of the phony owns. I was going with an up and coming actress and she kept dragging me to places where guys in red coats parked your car for you. The '56 Ford just didn't make it, pulling up at the Cocoanut Grove in '65. Everybody was embarrassed for us when we arrived, including her, which included me. I tried cleaning it up before these things, but that only seemed to make it more obvious, sort of like a bum in a new suit. I knew I had to get another car.

I had just started to play guitar and banjo behind Tom and Dick Smothers, and one night while we were playing a small folk club in Huntington Beach (rehearsing the act for Vegas), I asked Tommy if he'd loan me the money to make a down payment on a new car. He gave me a personal check right then and there for $600. The next night on the way to the club, I stopped off at a used car lot in Long Beach and bought a car to fit my future, a 1963, metallic silver-grey, 2-door Buick LeSabre hard-top convertible. It looked like a grey-haired executive.

The next day I drove over to my up and coming actress' place to show it off. She thought it was great, which I thought was great. Everything was just great, so I set about to get rid of the old Ford. I cleaned it out. Under the seats I found all kinds of stuff from all kinds of yesterdays — gas receipts, match-books, rodeo buttons, a piece of hair ribbon or two, lots of bobbie pins, a few dead bugs and some change. I ran back down through a few of our past adventures. Talked to it and patted it. I loved that car, we had rode a lot of poetry together. It was a buddy.

I had originally intended to sell it to a guy that ran a Texaco down the street, but my bass player didn't have a car, and since I was always having to go by and pick him up for gigs, and since I owed him a little money anyway, I just gave it to him. He took it and we split up shortly after that, so I don't know what happened to it, except him.

All of my friends told me a Buick LeSabre was exactly the wrong kind of car for me to own. But I was just getting into the big time fringes of show biz at that time, so I wasn't listening to my friends much. After my up and coming actress and I parted ways, I settled down to the confusion and didn't look up for a couple of years.

The Buick was good, I didn't love it or hate it, it was just right — it was a car. We left each other alone.

One time I was driving along behind a school bus, and it stopped, so I did too. (Stopping for a school bus is one of those special traffic laws you remember, I guess, because they make such a big thing out of it when you take your driver's license exam and you don't get to do it very often.) Anyway, the car behind me plowed into the back of me. It wasn't a bad one, I remember feeling interrupted more than anything else. I looked up in the rear view mirror at the car that had hit me. Steam and water were gushing out of the radiator. I turned back to look at the school bus. All the kids had run to the back window to see the accident. They were yelling and laughing and pointing, so I shot them the finger and made a funny face. They loved it and jeered some more. Then like a big, fat, yellow animal, the school bus lumbered off down the road.

I watched it for a minute, then got out. A little, middle-aged old lady was the driver of the car that hit me. She looked like our standard grandmother. I wasn't uptight at all, but she was in a complete dither. She knew the accident was her fault, and I guess all the implications were running through her Richard Hudnut. She was flitting all over the place like a scared canary, saying things like: "It's my fault . . . I should have . . . I just wasn't . . . I couldn't . . ." While she blithered on about her name, my name, our insurance companies, license numbers, taking the blame, her husband, lawsuits, the police and jail, I straightened out her fender so the tire would turn, picked up a few pieces of her car off the road, and more or less put things back together as much as possible. By the time I got through, she had spread all kinds of cards and identification out on her trunk for me to inspect. The whole incident was starting to get funny to me. I was loose, so I asked her if she'd feel better if we didn't report it. She said yes, that she knew it was her fault and that she would be glad to pay for any damage to my car, that we could surely exchange names and numbers and work this out in a civilized, satisfactory manner.

I decided to roll with it. I said, "Tell you what, let's just skip the whole thing." And she said, "But it was my fault! You stopped for a school bus and I hit you — Don't you want to have your car fixed?" And I said, "Naw, I never have cared too much for this car anyway, it'll serve it right." I kicked my car, which she thought was bizarre and if I'd a-had a hat, I'd a-tipped it. I got into my car, drove off and watched me disappear from her standing in the road in the center of my rear view mirror.

The Buick's silver-grey paint job perfectly matched the color of L.A.'s industrial sunrise. I was always coming home at dawn from girls and parties, and I used to have an image of it blending so much into the metallic morning that the car, like an invisible cloak, allowed me to move through the streets virtually unnoticed. This and the fact that the car had a lot of pep brought about a name: *The Silver Brisk,* which came from a poem I wrote one summer Sunday morning, after leaving a folk music picker's party in Pasadena and hitting a pigeon on the way home.

> Up the street I zoomed
> In the silver brisk of morning
> Past the silent houses
> Of summer Sunday sleeping
> In rooms cave cool and settled
> By the sedimental night

Where Mom and Dad
Sleep apart in their
Hard earned togetherness
And young couples
Hold on to each other until
Arms tingling
And thighs sweating
They have to break
For a breath of freedom
Before true love's
Next sleeping match

Where visitors huddle
On living room couches
With single blankets
And curse all night
The makeshift pillow
And rough upholstery

Where little girls
Of peaches and cream
Dream of tomorrow's tea party
In tin cups of imagination
With one lump or two
And little boys
Suspended from their real world
Of running and winning
Are beginning to venture
Away from their own backyard

There's never any extra
Parking places
On Sunday morning
Everybody's home asleep

The sun was only
A block from my house
When the pigeons
Started across the street
They always make it
So I gunned it
To keep them
On their pigeon toes
They took off in a flurry
But one with a crumb
Of something in its beak
Just didn't hurry . . . Boomph!

I saw feathers helter-skelter
In my rear view mirror
Like a pillow
Exploding under a dream

In February of 1967, I bought for the first time in my life a second car, an antique, a 1933 Pierce Arrow. I had been working in television the last ½ of '66 and the money was starting to roll in, so I was starting to roll it out.

The past summer, Ed Ruscha and I had gone out one evening on a sort of Da-Da Double Date. (I took Connie Stevens and he took somebody else.) We had dinner at a cafe on downtown L.A.'s Skid Row, visited a few strange places and just in general did what Connie Stevens would never do.

As transportation for the evening, we had rented a 1930 Chrysler touring car. It was beautiful bright yellow and lime green with a soft top. We rented it for 24 hours and between the two of us, drove it for most of the 24. It had a kind of magic power I had never even thought about a car having.

People in L.A. seem generally pretty indifferent to each other. This probably comes from the fact that L.A. is a car town, a big guinea pig for the automobile industry. You don't have to relate to people when you drive, you can think of them as cars. This experience of indifference probably feeds the over-all shitty-city attitude. Anyway, the Chrysler changed all that. As we drove around town, people yelled, waved, honked and pointed. The car broke down the barriers. Old men came up and told us old stories. Guys made us swapping deals at red lights. Beautiful girls blew us kisses from sportscars. Little kids yelled, "Hey! Who are you?" It was a breath away from the city attitude; you couldn't ignore us. We had a good thing and it made everybody else feel good.

Anyway, one day, Ed Ruscha called me and told me about an ad he'd found in the paper to sell a Pierce Arrow. I went out to look it over just for kicks and remembering what the Chrysler did to people, bought it. I figured a 1933 Pierce Arrow would probably be just as good as a '30 Chrysler to attitude around town in.

The guy who owned it had died, so his wife needed to sell it for the money. He had been working on it himself and it was about half-restored, with most of the mechanical work already done. It needed a paint job, upholstery and a few finishing touches to get it back in original shape. I didn't really have the time to work on it myself, I had just started writing for The Smothers Brothers Comedy Hour, so I had various people undertake the task of restoring it. It took about eighteen months to get it ready — it was hard to find good craftsmen who wanted to take the time to do it right.

In the meantime, while the Pierce Arrow was being restored, I took the Buick to work each morning and it brought me home each night. Tommy and I were living together at that time, because we were involved heavily with the Smothers Brother's Comedy Hour's attempt to be a little more aesthetically relevant on TV to people as people instead of as consumers, and with the CBS (Columbia Bowel System—Ha!) hassle. (After looking back, I think we were like a couple of kids who had flipped over a big rock and found the ugly truth about how television is really put together and why it is put together that way, and were innocently running around trying to tell people what we had discovered. "Hey, look at this big, ugly thing we found!")

We lived high up in the Hollywood Hills in a huge varnished, yellow wood, ski lodge-looking castle. Tom had 18 rooms and I had 7. When the Pierce was finally ready, there I sat high on the hog in Hollywood, a two car man in the middle of two extreme cars — a $10,000 concourse Pierce Arrow and a $600 passed-over executive banged-up Buick.

It was hard for me to drive the Pierce — I had made it too rich for my blood, but Tommy and I did manage to take it to a couple of Hollywood Award Presentations, a few jet set ditties and once or twice out Sunset Boulevard to the beach and back.

During the summer of 1968, I wrote the Glen Campbell summer replacement show for the Smothers Brothers, and also had my big hit "Classical Gas." I started getting more money, so I thought I'd get a career to go with my cars. I left the Smothers Brothers Show at the beginning of their last season on CBS (Cilly Bland Stuff—Ha²!) to pursue life, liberty and justice for all. Amen.

I rented a whole house of my own, put the Pierce Arrow in the garage and began to live a little wider, less wilder life on the side. I got over being afraid of driving the Pierce Arrow because it was too nice and started to enjoy it.

I had picked up a pretty good case of Don Quixote from the Smothers Brothers censorship hassle and it drew me deeper into a philosophic reality, an idealistic integrity about ideas and myself. I liked the Smothers Brothers Comedy Hour's flavor. I liked being on the good ideas side, so I decided to keep trying to play it well and not just wealthy. I wanted to have some say-so about how what I did was used. I worked in the medium of not doing. I felt that anybody who used their talent for TV was like a Werner Von Braun making good rockets for Hitler. I thought the best I could do was not at all for TV.

I started using the Pierce as a teaching aid for my philosophy. I'd take people for rides in it and talk about the quality, the craftsmanship and the love put into it, about how it represented the direction technology absolutely didn't go. I'd say, "If American technology is so great, how come they couldn't figure out how to do more of this idea cheaper instead of losing it altogether?"

I used it one time on my music publisher to explain why I didn't want "Classical Gas" to be used for a TV commercial for a gasoline company. We went for a ride in it and I told him I didn't care for the way American business used people's ideas and hard work for our mutual destruction. I pointed out to him that the "rich" look of the Pierce Arrow was secondary to its real attraction, that the whole concept of quality, rich or poor, is an antique now and that the craftsmanship and hand-made care, the respect built into it was what people really liked about it. He turned down the offer — a loss of $30,000 to both of us. He said he dug it.

The Buick was getting a little shoddy in the body, so I decided it was time to buy another car. Having been around show biz, I picked up the life-tab habit and went right on with it. I asked my accountant what the best, nice car was for the money and whatever it was, please get me a new one. On New Year's Day, I was delivered a brand new 1969 Mercedes 280-SL 2-seater hard-top convertible Sports Coupé. It was the same color green as my Pierce Arrow — English Racing. Now I had a set, a big old one and a little new one.

The Mercedes is a beautiful machine. Fantastically engineered and precise, like a fine watch. The big thing I noticed about it is its feel, the flavor of its performance and ride. It's one of those experiences you didn't know existed, a whole other approach. The first time I drove it, I felt the same way I did about the first French cuisine I had; I didn't even know such a dimension of the concept was possible. If there is ever any doubt about "the giant conspiracy," these kind of moments cause it. "How come there ain't no American cars that ride like this? How come I had to get rich to find out this flavor existed? Who owns all the opportunities to feel what's possible?"

Since 1964, I had been a behind-the-scenes-performer, a writer, a composer and so on, but I went back on the road in March of '69 to do college and symphony concerts, to once again become a barker for myself.

We flew commercial airlines at first, but afterwhile I found it impossible to fly anywhere and be in a good enough frame of mind by concert time to do a good show. (The Airline Business is one of the great ugliness barometers of corporate America's progross.) I finally realized that my attitude *is* my music, and in order to feel good so the music would, I had to skip the kitchy nouveau richy motel room vibes that the corporate piggies have forced on us (and their employees) via airlines. We went by Greyhound Bus as much as possible. Greyhound hasn't kept up with the times, much to its credit, or I should say, much to *their* credit, the people in the company, and especially the drivers. (If you ever want to organize a team of good guy commandos to turn the tide and make everything right and beautiful, you wouldn't go wrong to choose Greyhound drivers.) They and the bus made the music better.

We traveled all over America and played for all kinds of people. Seeing it as a whole, and somewhat condensed and edited by the speed of our one nighterness, my attitude toward the whole commotion of car going has changed. I saw us as we really are — a nation of motorized lemmings in high gear, running for the sea.

Freedom of the road in America used to stand for the freedom to come and go as you please, when and wherever. But now the whole country's enslaved to that freedom. We can't stop. We're like a race horse shot full of speed to make us run harder than is good for us, to win for the owners and lose for ourselves, to win the race for only the price of the chance to run.

The road used to feel like a wide stretch of pretty good nothing to roll along on, but it doesn't feel that way now. The open road is closing, and I think maybe we're selling it out by buying it. Take the Interstate Highways, for example, but not just as the road, as the idea of it, the motive behind it, the reason for it. I, and I think probably most of the American people, more or less think of it as being a super vacation good time highway, but after zooming down several thousand miles of it, you begin to get a deeper, hidden bad flavor, that good old military waste taste.

It probably is a military highway — it's bleak enough. Somebody once told me it's a bad idea defense-wise, it completely destroys our natural defense, the terrain, which is often a country's best defense (a la Viet Nam). They said, if we were ever invaded, an enemy could get to us everywhere really quick, the same way we got to Berlin on Hitler's Autobaun at the end of World War II. However, I'm sure the military counts on an enemy taking the wrong off ramp or something like that. Anyway, I don't care how good or bad a defense idea it is, I just don't like military flavor. I don't like riding their roads, it's like eating their food and wearing their clothes, once again it just gets you there.

The big reason I don't like the flavor of Freeways and Interstates is that in their planning, they only take economics into consideration, never people. They have destroyed thousands of Americans by destroying their opportunity to be so, their opportunity to have a business and therefore a life that reflects their own unique flavor. They've taken us right past us, not to us. We are traditionally romantic in this country, and the Freeways and Interstates have literally by-passed our romantic tradition of individuality, which is and soon to be, was, the generating source of our freedom.

There is always room for more subtle deceit and we have literally paved the way for it in the case of our Great Highway System. The roads are so good, people drive on them more than they would normally. Freeways and Interstates are paid for by us to accommodate the use of the Automobile Industry's products way beyond what is sane. They've become exactly what they were created to overcome. They're a convenience carried to the point of inconvenience. They're time savers that one spends more time on saving than one would ordinarily even spend saving.

As for smog, I think it chokes for itself, so I won't go into it much, thank you, except to point up another little ironic example of the two-faced advantages we're supposedly getting from our progress.

I live in Los Angeles and I've noticed that if it's a beautiful day, everybody immediately jumps into their car to go out and enjoy it, and smogs it to death. I'm beginning to hate beautiful mornings, because I know they're going to end up ugly afternoons.

L.A. DAY

I look out the window
As the day goes by
Watching the progress
Screw up the sky

One piece of logic that's always bothered me about roads concerns the neighborhood street. When they build a new neighborhood, the sewers and drain pipes go under the pavement and in a few years, when the sewers or drains need repair, they dig up the streets, fix them and then patch them up nice and badly with big bumps and chuck holes. Why don't they put the pipes beside the street, or at least under the gutter?

Maybe I'm being overly suspicious, but if I am, it's probably because I've been running around in my car too much, isolated from other people, which tends to make you suspicious. The automobile and the TV set have probably done more to make us afraid or suspicious of each other than anything else. When we walked and talked to each other on the street, each other was a familiar experience. But isolation is good for business. It takes a lot of money and blind energy to get the stuff you need to keep yourself away from all those other people. Anyway, the question being: Who benefits most from bumpy streets? The answer being: The Automobile Industry, whose products bumpy streets tear up and wear out faster.

I might be wrong about this, but that would be just right for what's going on. The people who own America like for you to be wrong, or at least feel wrong, because there's nothing juicyer for making money than to get a whole bunch of nice people who want to do what's right, intimidate them with guilt, which is to make them feel wrong, whether they are or not, so you can wipe out their natural sense of what's right and sell your own brand of what's right back to them as their own. Guilt causes you a mental blindness, so someone else can lead you around.

The whole simple concept of going places in a car has become infected with ulterior psychological labyrinths designed to intimidate and robotize us for purposes of control. I suspect the reasoning is: If you'll buy a lot of dumb rules, you'll also buy a lot of dumb products.

I notice more and more that when I'm driving, I have in the back of my mind a constant little feeling of guilt, or more specifically, I have a constant little doubt about my innocence. If I see a police car, I automatically feel guilty. I slow down, look around, try to act normal. My guilt, I realize, comes from the fact that I break a few little traffic laws from time to time, which are absurd in many cases, and which there are too many of in any case. (That's how you break people down and control them, give them a labyrinth of too many little rules with some dumb one mixed in with the good ones and they'll, afterwhile, break all the dumb ones because they're easy and in fact, natural to break, and pick up that good old guilt from breaking them without realizing it. Organized religion has done this for centuries. It, too, has a lot of little moral traffic laws that are easy and in fact, natural to break.

Traffic law seems to have become more than a framework of rules for the trafficking of automobiles, there seems to be a little ulterior motive tacked onto it nowadays. They've gotten into the swing of things and become another maze of confusion for taking away the individual's experience of self-motivation.

Many towns, especially smaller ones, are traffic concentration camps. They have so many direction signs, lights and yellow lines that the people don't ever have a moment when they figure things out for themselves. To go through Eugene, Oregon, for example, is like going through a game of hop-scotch designed to break your leg. My mother, who lives close to there, told me that they change all the one-way street signs and stuff from time to time to make it even more confusing. It makes you wonder if all the signs, and there are a lot of them and expensive ones too, aren't perhaps creating the problems they solve. That's probably what's going on, people have always been suckers for the same old trick — If it causes a lot of trouble, it must be worth doing.

So many one-way streets to me point to only one thing, that somebody wants to take our individual motivation away. Somebody for some reason wants to intimidate us to the point of where we don't remember how to think and do for ourselves anymore, where we just obey the rules without question, or if not, cause ourselves the ever-popular, life-crippling guilt which makes us finally have to obey the rules after all out of fear. (They get you one way or the other.) Somebody, somewhere, for some reason, is trying to cause us a need we don't need. I think we've become a junkie nation and the auto industry's the pusher. We've all got a piece or two of their junk in our driveway.

The obvious is obviously not so obvious anymore, that we're all operators of the Automobile Industry's product, and they've got us working for them on our own time.

I just sold my little Mercedes — nothing wrong with it — I just don't want it anymore. I'll hang onto the Pierce Arrow for what little getting around I might need to do, but I'm going to try to quit driving for the Automobile Industry. I'm going to get going and leave them behind. I'm going to walk where I can, take the bus, skip it, or ride a bicycle — at least until they make it a law for you to own a car and drive it, which

I'm sure they're working on. Besides, the police make me nervous now, I guess because they're nervous. I'm starting to get the feeling that my driver's license is becoming my papers. I've always stayed out of bars to avoid trouble, so I'll just stay out of cars, too.

My step-father used to say that Americans would rather go and blow than do anything else. I guess he was right — your attitude always becomes your product, you reap just what you sow.

Sow, here I sit in the promised land with a great way to go, and wouldn't you know it, it ain't no fun to go anymore. To go now is to blow it — ain't that rich?

UNLAWFUL TO READ THIS SIGN

THE
OUTTA SIGHT
LIGHT SHOW

A NATURAL PSYCHEDELIC VISUAL EXPERIENCE

HERE'S WHAT YOU NEED

A. ONE SODA STRAW

B. ONE B-B SHOT

C. ONE SLIDE WHISTLE

D. ONE WOODBLOCK AND WHACKER

E. TWO PALS (OR MOM AND DAD)

STEP 1. TWIST ONE END OF SODA
       STRAW. (FIG. 1)

FIG. 1

STEP 2. HOLD STRAW WITH
       TWISTED END DOWN.
       DROP B-B SHOT INTO
       OPEN END OF SODA
       STRAW.

STEP 3. AFTER B-B HITS BOTTOM
       CRIMP SODA STRAW
       WITH THUMB AND
←CRIMP INDEX FINGER
       DIRECTLY ABOVE
←B-B   B-B. (THIS TRAPS
       THE B-B BETWEEN
       THE TWIST AND THE
←TWIST CRIMP.) (FIG. 2)

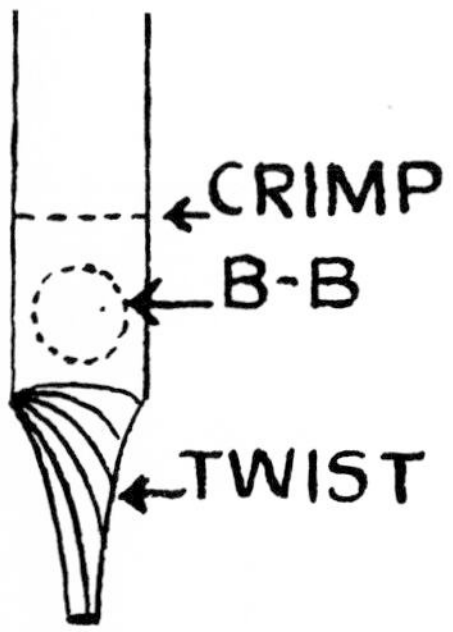

FIG. 2

STEP 4. GIVE SLIDE WHISTLE TO
ONE PAL AND WOODBLOCK
AND WHACKER TO THE
OTHER.

CAUTION:

REMOVE ALL EYEGLASSES
OR CONTACT LENSES.

NOW
YOU ARE READY
TO EXPERIENCE

THE
OUTTA SIGHT
LIGHT SHOW

STEP 5. HOLD STRAW CLOSE
TO EITHER EYE. TILT
HEAD BACK AND LOOK
UP INTO OPEN END OF
SODA STRAW. (FIG. 3)

FIG. 3

STEP 6. HAVE PAL WITH WOOD-
BLOCK COUNT DOWN
FROM 10 TO 0.

STEP 7. AT ZERO, UNCRIMP STRAW,
RELEASING B-B SHOT.
AS B-B DROPS DOWN SODA
STRAW, PAL WITH SLIDE
WHISTLE PLAYS A FAST
HIGH-TO-LOW-PULL-AND-BLOW
"SLURP" NOTE.

STEP 8. AS B-B HITS EYEBALL,
SLIDE WHISTLE "SLURP"
NOTE SHOULD END AND
WOODBLOCK SHOULD BE
STRUCK BY PAL WITH
WHACKER.

You'll see...

BLUE STARS YELLOW FLASHES AND RED SPOTS

RIGHT BEFORE YOUR VERY EYE WHICH IS

OUT'TA SIGHT!

MY ACT

In my act
I don't have things to remember
I have things to do
In fact
I don't even have an act
I just act like I do

THE FORM OF DOING

First you just do it
Then you do it for fun
Then you seriously do it
And then you're done

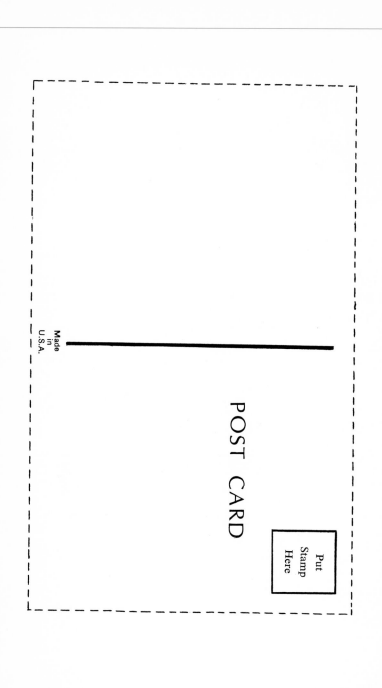

POST CARD

Made
in
U.S.A.

Put
Stamp
Here

☐ THE INTELLIGENT STUPIDITY TEST

☐ *Mark the correct answer.*

☐ Intelligence is intelligent.
☐ Intelligence is stupid.
☐ Stupidity is intelligent.
☐ Stupidity is stupid.
☐ None of the above.
☐ One of the above.
☐ All of the above.
☐ Some of the above.
☐ This one.
☐ Does not apply.
☐ Yes.
☐ No.
☐ Yes and no.
☐ I don't know.
☐ . . . uh.
☐ Ignorance is no excuse.
☐ ☒
☐ ☐
☐
☐ ————————————————.
☐ ——————————————————————————.
☐ etc.

☐ (See answer next page)

□ THE INTELLIGENT STUPIDITY TEST

□ *Mark the correct answer.*

□ Intelligence is intelligent.
□ Intelligence is stupid.
□ Stupidity is intelligent.
□ Stupidity is stupid.
□ None of the above.
□ One of the above.
□ All of the above.
□ Some of the above.
□ This one.
□ Does not apply.
□ Yes.
□ No.
□ Yes and no.
□ I don't know.
□ . . . uh.
□ Ignorance is no excuse.
□ ☒
□ □
□
□ _____.
□ _____.
□ etc.

GOODBYE
RENO ST.

GOODBYE RENO ST.

When I was a kid
I never could handle
The full force of Reno St.

I only went down there
For second hand auto parts
Leather, rope or tools
To see real mythical prostitutes
And never alone at night

I was afraid to go in
Most of those places
Afraid to look into
Anybody's face
I was afraid to touch
Anybody or anything

I know now
Why you scared me
When I was a kid, Reno St.
You were
The raw power of life
Caught in the act of being

Life has always been
An eyesore to society

So goodbye
Bargain Sin Center
Of Oklahoma City History
As I say
Safely from this paper
Goodbye, Reno St.

We always drink the whole bottle of beer
Ride with the radio on
Join all the clubs
Use everything up as fast as we can
I knew you'd read this whole page

Our history's in our news
Our history's in our magazines
Our history's in our trash

THE DRAFT

The Draft
Is like a drunk at a party
You want to stay away from if possible
Your life is a delicate opportunity
And you just know he's going to bump into you
And spill it

← Dirt →
↓

DEFINITIONS[3]

Things Defining Themselves
As Themselves
In the Form Of Themselves

TIME

Everything is made out of time
Time is the how of all of what is done
Time makes everything by hand
Even itself
The universe is hand made time
It's a form within a form in the same form
It takes time time to be time
And time takes the time to be time

FREEDOM

The idea of freedom
Automatically enslaves you
True freedom is not being aware
Of freedom as an idea

Even the word freedom
Is not free
It must be spelled
F-R-E-E-D-O-M everytime

Freedom should be free
In order to be
What it is, which is:

VOID

Void is da woid
Dat voids
Da concept of void
By being da woid
Dat voids it

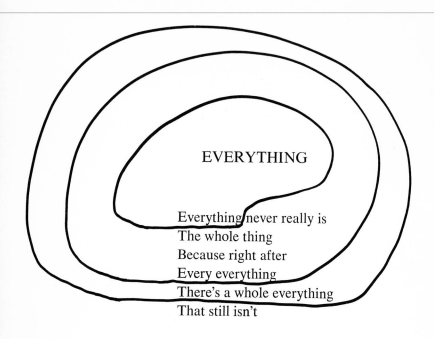

EVERYTHING

Everything never really is
The whole thing
Because right after
Every everything
There's a whole everything
That still isn't

And look it under
If you run it upon the rack
You can understand anything
Stand under it and see what makes it run
To understand something is to

TO UNDERSTAND

NOW

Now was right then
When it was
And here it comes again
Right then

GOD

W
GOD
R
D

THE TOP

Your eyes have to look at the top
For your mind to see what it is
Therefore,
You'll never reach
The very top, because
Your mind's in the way

THE END

(See answer last page)

SWEET
FLORIO

FLORIO & C.

REG. U. S. PAT. OFF.

MARSALA

SUPERIOR EXTRA MARSALA

CONTENTS 1 PT. - 6 FLD OZ. - ALCOHOL 18% BY VOLUME
Produced and Bottled at MARSALA (Sicily) ITALY

PRINTED IN ITALY

By *Florio & C.*

· *Established 1833* ·
SOC per AZ. VINICOLA ITALIANA
MARSALA · ITALY

GIACALONE - MARSALA

SOLE UNITED STATES DISTRIBUTORS
Schieffelin & Co. - New York
IMPORTERS SINCE 1794

Pour a little bit of this stuff on some vanilla ice creme and
see if you like it.

Which came first, the chicken or the egg?

The question.